# THE ATLANTA BRAVES

Sloan MacRae

**PowerKiDS** press
New York

Published in 2012 by The Rosen Publishing Group, Inc.
29 East 21st Street, New York, NY 10010

First Edition

Editor: Amelie von Zumbusch
Book Design: Greg Tucker
Layout Design: Ashley Drago

Photo Credits: Cover (background) Al Messerschmidt/Getty Images; cover (Jason Heyward), p. 21 Ezra Shaw/Getty Images; cover (Hank Aaron), pp. 13, 15, 22 (left) Rogers Photo Archive/Getty Images; cover (Warren Spahn), p. 11 Photo File/Hulton Archive/Getty Images; p. 5 Mitchell Layton/Getty Images; p. 7 Mike Zarrilli/Getty Images; p. 9 Bruce Bennett Studios/Getty Images; p. 17 George Gojkovich/Getty Images; pp. 19, 22 (bottom) Ronald C. Modra/Getty Images.

Library of Congress Cataloging-in-Publication Data

MacRae, Sloan.
  The Atlanta Braves / by Sloan MacRae. — 1st ed.
     p. cm. — (America's greatest teams)
  Includes index.
  ISBN 978-1-4488-5007-5 (library binding) — ISBN 978-1-4488-5147-8 (pbk.) —
  ISBN 978-1-4488-5148-5 (6-pack)
  1. Atlanta Braves (Baseball team)—History—Juvenile literature. I. Title.
  GV875.A8M47 2012
  796.357'6409758231—dc22
                                    2010050103

Manufactured in the United States of America

CPSIA Compliance Information: Batch #WS11PK: For Further Information contact Rosen Publishing, New York, New York at 1-800-237-9932

# CONTENTS

# AMERICA'S TEAM

Baseball is often called America's national sport, and the Atlanta Braves are often called America's Team. The Braves are America's Team because they have so many fans all across the United States. Baseball is one of the oldest American sports, and the Braves are one of the oldest **franchises** in baseball. This rich history also makes them America's Team. Many of the greatest hitters and **pitchers** of all time have been Braves.

The Braves have not always played in Atlanta, Georgia. They were once based in Boston, Massachusetts, and later in Milwaukee, Wisconsin. America's Team has won **championships** for three different American cities!

Brian McCann started catching for the Braves in 2005. He won a Silver Slugger Award as catcher in 2006, 2008, 2009, and 2010.

# TURNER FIELD

Today the Braves play in the city of Atlanta. Their **stadium** is called Turner Field. It is named after businessman Ted Turner. He used to be the Braves' owner. Sometimes Turner Field is called the Home of the Braves.

The Braves' colors are navy blue, white, and red. The team's players wear the letter *A* for "Atlanta" on their hats. The Braves get their name from strong Native American fighters. The most important American sports teams all have special signs called **logos**. The Braves' logo is a picture of a **tomahawk** underneath their name. A tomahawk is an old Native American weapon.

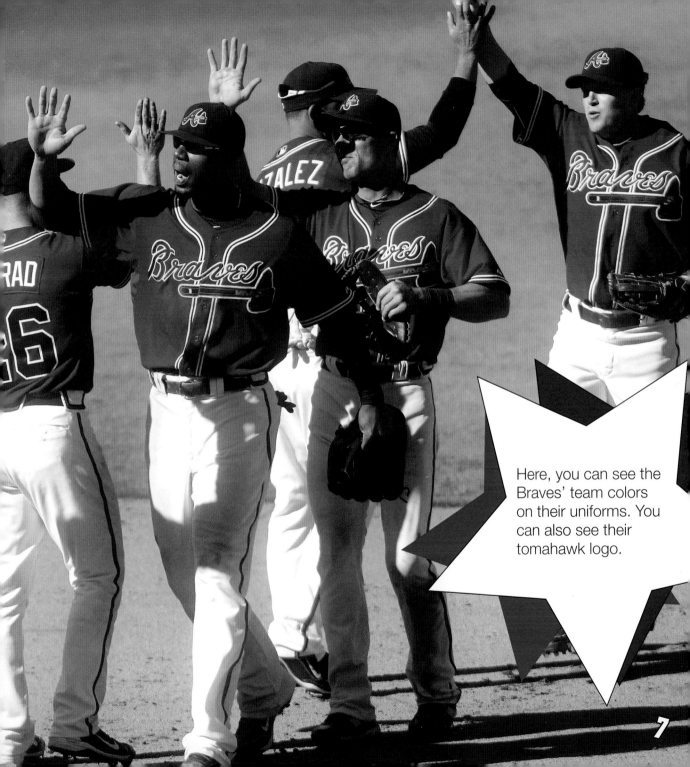

Here, you can see the Braves' team colors on their uniforms. You can also see their tomahawk logo.

# THE MIRACLE IN BOSTON

The Braves' history began in Boston in 1871. The team was called the Boston Red Stockings. The Red Stockings got off to a strong start. They quickly won six **pennants**.

The team changed its name several times in its early years. They settled on the Braves in 1912. Their new name did not bring them any luck at first. They struggled in 1912 and 1913. The 1914 season started off slowly, too. Then star players, such as Johnny Evers, turned the team around. They led the Braves to win their first **World Series**! The 1914 team became known as the **Miracle** Braves.

Hank Gowdy, seen here, was one of the stars of the Miracle Braves. Other stars included Evers, Rabbit Maranville, Butch Schmidt, and Dick Rudolph.

# SPAHN AND SAIN

The Braves struggled in the 1920s and early 1930s. They made a deal to bring Babe Ruth to the team in 1935. Ruth was baseball's biggest star at that time. However, he played for only part of that season before quitting baseball forever. Before he retired, Ruth hit his 714th **home run**. This set a record that stood until another Brave broke it years later.

The Braves returned to greatness in the 1940s behind the pitching of Warren Spahn and Johnny Sain. Spahn and Sain even helped the Braves make it to the 1948 World Series. They lost to the Cleveland Indians, though.

Warren Spahn stayed with the Braves until 1964. He won 363 games during his long career.

11

# MILWAUKEE

The Braves were not the only baseball team in Boston. The Boston Red Sox were also a great team. In fact, the Red Sox had more fans than the Braves. The Braves' owners began to look for a new home for the team. They decided on Milwaukee. The team moved there in 1953.

The people of Milwaukee loved baseball. They were very happy to finally have a **major-league** team. When the city threw a parade for the new Milwaukee Braves, 60,000 people showed up. The Braves played very well in their new town. They were once again one of the hottest teams in baseball.

In Milwaukee, the Braves played in Milwaukee County Stadium. During the 1953 season, nearly two million fans watched the Braves play there.

# HAMMERIN' HANK

Baseball changed forever when Henry "Hank" Aaron took the field for the Braves in 1954. Aaron went on to break some of baseball's biggest records. Many fans believe he is the greatest player in the history of baseball. Aaron was so good at hitting home runs that his teammates nicknamed him Hammerin' Hank. Pitchers on other teams hated pitching to him, so they called him Bad Henry.

Aaron and Spahn led the Braves to the World Series in 1957. Aaron hit three home runs in the series. The rest of the team played well, too. The Braves beat the Yankees, four games to three.

Hank Aaron was named the National League's most valuable player, or MVP, for his part in the Braves' great 1957 season.

# ATLANTA AND NUMBER 715

The Braves struggled to match the success of their 1957 season. They were still a good team. However, they were no longer the best in baseball. Many Milwaukee fans lost interest in them. The Braves' owners decided to move the team to a bigger city. The Braves headed to Atlanta in 1966. They played very well for their new fans.

Hank Aaron finished the 1973 season with 713 home runs. Everyone knew that he would break Babe Ruth's record sometime in the following year. It did not take him long. He hit home run number 715 just a few days into the 1974 season.

Aaron played with great teammates, such as pitcher Phil Niekro. Niekro was known for his knuckleball, which was very hard to hit.

# THE TEAM OF THE 90S

The Braves struggled again in the late 1980s. They gave fans lots of reasons to cheer in the 1990s, though. Atlanta built a great team around young pitchers Tom Glavine, John Smoltz, and Steve Avery. Chipper Jones became one of the best hitters in baseball. Star pitcher Greg Maddux joined the team in 1993. The Braves reached the World Series in 1995. They faced the Cleveland Indians, as they had in 1948. This time, though, the Braves came out on top.

The Braves were baseball's best team during the 1990s. They set a record by becoming the champions of their **division** 14 years in a row.

Here, pitcher Mark Wohlers cheers after the Braves won the 1995 World Series. The Braves' pitchers played a big part in their win.

# BATTING BACK

In 2006, the Braves failed to win their division for the first time since 1990. It was still a good season for them, though. The Braves set several more records. The Braves had been on top of baseball for a long time, but now that time was over. Even with great players like Chipper Jones and Brian McCann, the Braves failed to reach the **postseason** for the next three years.

They fought back in 2010 and reached the National League Division Series. Many of the greatest players in baseball continue to play for the Braves. Stars such as Brian McCann, Martín Prado, and Jason Heyward will keep America's Team winning.

Jason Heyward joined the Braves in 2010. He had a great rookie, or first, season. He hit a home run his first time at bat!

# ATLANTA BRAVES TIMELINE

**1912**

The Boston Braves take the field with their new name.

**1876**

The Boston Red Stockings play their first National League game. They beat the Philadelphia Athletics.

**1914**

The Miracle Braves sweep the Philadelphia Athletics to win their first World Series.

**1954**

Hank Aaron plays his first game with the Milwaukee Braves.

**1948**

The Braves lose the World Series to the Cleveland Indians.

**1935**

Babe Ruth retires from baseball after hitting a record 714 home runs.

**1974**

Hank Aaron hits his 715th home run and breaks Babe Ruth's world record.

**1966**

The team plays its first game as the Atlanta Braves.

**1957**

The Milwaukee Braves beat the New York Yankees in the World Series.

**1995**

The Braves beat the Cleveland Indians and win their third World Series.

# GLOSSARY

**CHAMPIONSHIPS** (CHAM-pee-un-ships)  Contests held to determine the best, or the winner.

**DIVISION** (dih-VIH-zhun)  A group of teams that play against each other.

**FRANCHISES** (FRAN-chyz-ez)  Teams that are part of a professional group.

**HOME RUN** (HOHM RUN)  A hit in which the batter touches all the bases and scores a run.

**LOGOS** (LOH-gohz)  Pictures, words, or letters that stand for a team or company.

**MAJOR-LEAGUE** (MAY-jur-leeg)  Having to do with a group of baseball teams made up of the best players.

**MIRACLE** (MEER-uh-kul)  A wonderful or an unexpected event.

**PENNANTS** (PEH-nunts)  League championships.

**PITCHERS** (PIH-cherz)  Players who throw the ball for people to hit in baseball.

**POSTSEASON** (pohst-SEE-zun)  Games played after the regular season.

**STADIUM** (STAY-dee-um)  A place where sports are played.

**TOMAHAWK** (TO-mih-hawk)  A kind of ax that some Native Americans used as a weapon.

**WORLD SERIES** (WURLD SEER-eez)  A group of games in which the two best baseball teams play against each other.

# INDEX

# WEB SITES

Due to the changing nature of Internet links, PowerKids Press has developed an online list of Web sites related to the subject of this book. This site is updated regularly. Please use this link to access the list:
www.powerkidslinks.com/agt/braves/